Pumpkins

Victoria Blakemore

Copyright info/picture credits

Cover, Sandra Cunningham/AdobeStock; Page 3, Capri23auto/Pixabay; Page 5, nikles5/Pixabay; Page 7, Sandra Cunningham/AdobeStock; Page 9, Ruud Morijn/AdobeStock; Page 11, Nayuta/Pixabay; Page 13, Denise/AdobeStock; Page 15, Alliance/AdobeStock; Page 17, Elena/AdobeStock; Page 19, stealth_sly/Pixabay; Page 21, Pexels/Pixabay; Page 23; gayulo/Pixabay; Page 25, Storyblocks; Page 27, pololia/AdobeStock; Page 29, wisutapron/AdobeStock; Page 31, Engin_Akyurt/Pixabay; Page 33, StockSnap/Pixabay; Page 35, BillionPhotos.com/AdobeStock; Page 37, pgbsimon/Pixabay

Table of Contents

What Are Pumpkins?

Pumpkins are members of the **gourd** family. Other members of this family include squash and zucchini.

Most pumpkins that you see are orange. Pumpkins actually come in many different colors.

They can also be green, yellow, white, blue, red, or a mix of colors.

Size

Pumpkins come in many shapes and sizes. Some can be as small as three inches across. They can weigh less than two pounds.

Many pumpkins that are sold in stores are between five and twenty pounds.

The largest pumpkin on record weighed 2,624 pounds. It was grown in Belgium in 2016.

History of Pumpkins

Pumpkins were first grown in the Americas. Some Native Americans would roast strips of pumpkin over the fire.

Christopher Columbus is said to have brought pumpkin seeds back to Europe. The Pilgrims grew many pumpkins because they stored well for winter.

The word pumpkin comes

from a Greek word that

means "large melon."

Pumpkin Vines

Pumpkin vines grow from pumpkin seeds. They can grow very fast and very long.

Vines are made up of one main vine with lots of smaller pieces that grow off of it. These pieces are sometimes called runners.

The vine brings **nutrients** and water from the soil to the pumpkins.

Pumpkin Skin

Pumpkin skin is the outer layer of the pumpkin. It is also called the **rind**.

The pumpkin skin protects the inside parts of a pumpkin. It keeps the seeds safe from weather and being eaten by animals.

Some scientists are studying pumpkin skins. They believe that parts of the skins can be used to make medicine.

Pumpkin Flesh

The pumpkin flesh is the hard part of the pumpkin just under the skin. It can also be called the meat of the pumpkin.

Pumpkin flesh can be cooked many ways. It can be boiled, roasted, steamed, and baked.

Pumpkin flesh is hard until it is

cooked.

Pumpkin Seeds

Pumpkin seeds are dark green. In some kinds of pumpkins, the seeds are inside cream colored husks.

The pumpkin seeds are found inside the pumpkin. They are in an orange mixture called pulp.

Pumpkin seeds are often saved when pumpkins are carved. The seeds can be roasted for a snack.

Pumpkin Pulp

The pulp is the stringy, sticky mixture inside the pumpkin. The pulp holds the seeds together inside the pumpkin.

Like the flesh and the seeds, the pulp is also edible. Many people do not eat the pulp because of the sticky **texture**.

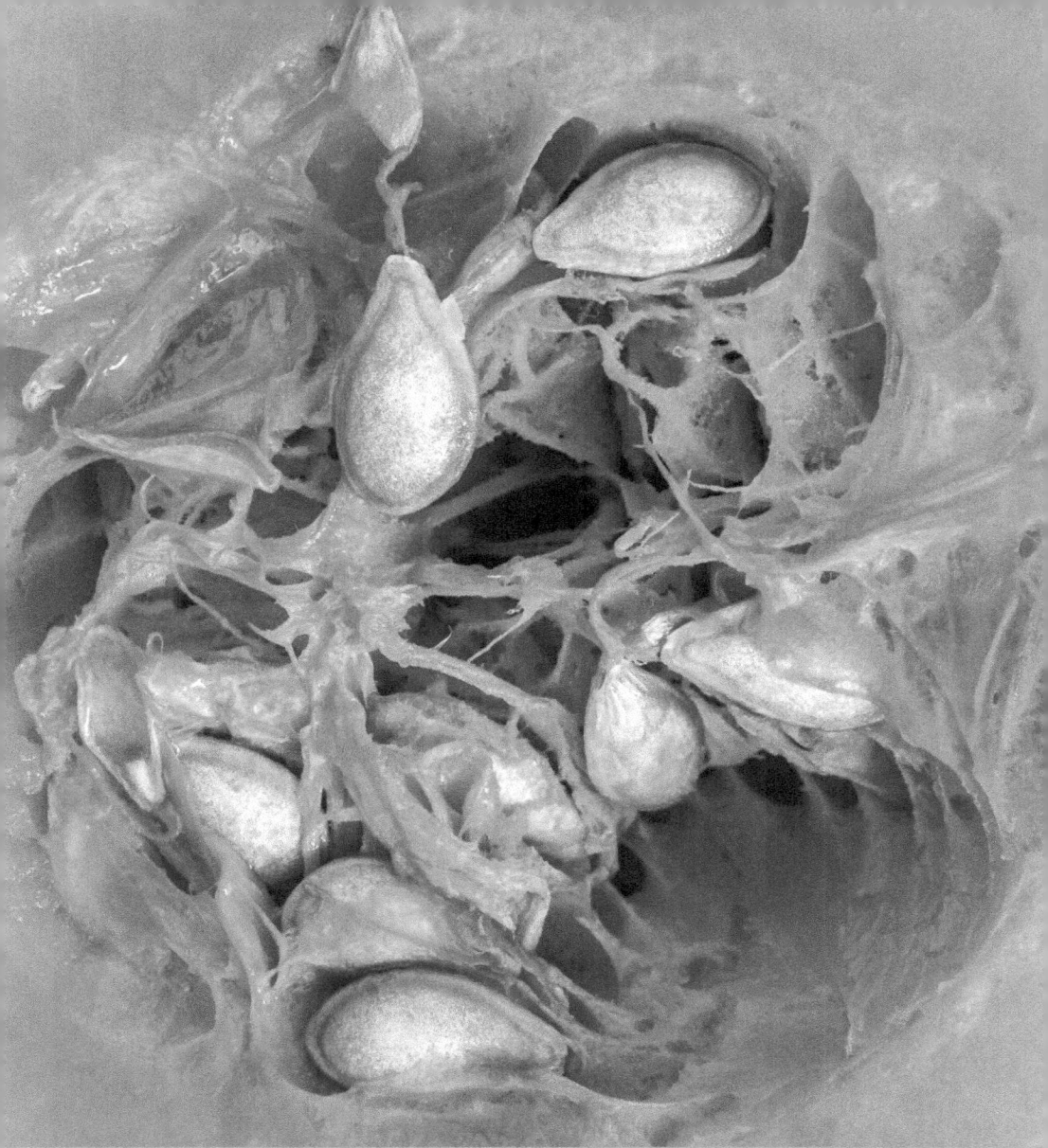

When carving a pumpkin,

the pulp and seeds must be

removed.

Life Cycle

First, a pumpkin seed is be

planted in soil. With enough

water, nutrients, and sunlight,

it will grow into a sprout.

The sprouts will grow into vines.

When the vines are big

enough, they grow yellow

flowers.

If they are **pollinated**, the flowers will grow into pumpkins. The pumpkin contain the seeds needed to grow new pumpkins.

19

Where Are Pumpkins Grown?

Pumpkins are grown in many different countries. China grows more pumpkins each year than any other country.

Pumpkins are grown on every continent except Antarctica. Most are grown in Asia and Europe.

In the United States, Illinois

produces the most pumpkins

out of all of the states.

Growing Pumpkins

Pumpkin seeds are usually planted in early July. This means that they will be ready to harvest by late September.

The seeds need to be planted at least five feet apart. This is because the vines grow very long. They need to have enough space to grow.

Pumpkins are usually grown in large fields. These fields are called pumpkin patches.

Pumpkins are **ripe** and ready to be harvested by September or October.

Pumpkins that are grown to be made into pies or pie filling may be harvested by machines. Pumpkins that are going to be for sale are usually harvested by hand.

Pumpkins that are harvested by

hand are less likely to be

bruised or damaged.

Transportation

Pumpkins are often transported to stores in large bins. They are packed carefully to keep the pumpkins from getting bruised.

When the pumpkins are going to be sold **locally**, they may be transported with a tractor.

Tractors can pull trailers with heavy loads. They make it easy to move pumpkins from one place to another.

Selling Pumpkins

Pumpkins are sold in many grocery stores and markets in the fall.

Some farms let people pick their own pumpkin. People come to the field and choose the pumpkin right from the vine.

In the fall, many pumpkins are
sold from roadside stands and
farmer's markets.

Nutrition

Pumpkins are very good for you.

They provide your body with

nutrients such as potassium,

beta-carotene, calcium, and

vitamin A.

Pumpkin seeds have a lot of

nutrients too. They are full of

protein, iron, and vitamin B.

Cooked pumpkin is low in calories. Pumpkin seeds are higher in calories because of all of their protein.

Health Benefits

The nutrients in pumpkins can help you to stay healthy.

Beta-carotene and vitamin A can help you to have good eyesight and keep you from getting sick. Potassium can help to keep your heart and kidneys healthy.

Eating Pumpkins

People use pumpkins for several different kinds of food. Pies, bread, and soup are some popular pumpkin foods.

Roasted pumpkin seeds are also a popular snack. Coffees are often flavored with pumpkin spices in the fall.

Pumpkin pie is a popular dessert during autumn, especially on Thanksgiving.

Other Uses for Pumpkins

Pumpkins have other uses than just food. They can be made into creams and scrubs for skin care.

Pumpkins are often used as decorations for autumn and Halloween. They can be used inside or outside to celebrate the season.

Many people carve faces or
pictures into the pumpkins to
make jack-o-lanterns.

Glossary

Bruise: a dark spot on fruit that may be softer than the rest of the fruit

Gourd: round fruits that are related to the squash

Locally: close by

Nutrients: something in food that helps people, animals, and plants grow

Pollinated: when pollen is moved from one plant to another, allowing crops to grow

Produces: makes, grows

Rind: the tough outer layer of a pumpkin

Ripe: ready to be eaten

Texture: how something feels

About the Author

Victoria Blakemore is a first grade

teacher in Southwest Florida with a

passion for reading.

You can visit her at

www.elementaryexplorers.com

Also in This Series

Gray Wolves	Sloths	Flamingos	Camels	Koalas	Honey Bees
Pandas	Pangolins	White-Tailed Deer	Orcas	Giraffes	Corn
Meerkats	Echidnas	Walruses	Raccoons	Bald Eagles	Apples
Arctic Foxes	Red Pandas	Cassowaries	Tigers	Ladybugs	Moose
Beluga Whales	Leopards	Elephants	Jellyfish	Binturongs	Lions
Dolphins	Reindeer	Hammerhead Sharks	Hippos	Pumpkins	Peafowl

Elementary Explorers

Victoria Blakemore

Also in This Series

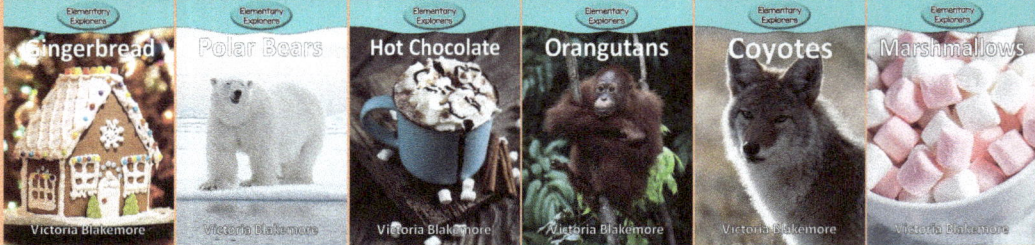

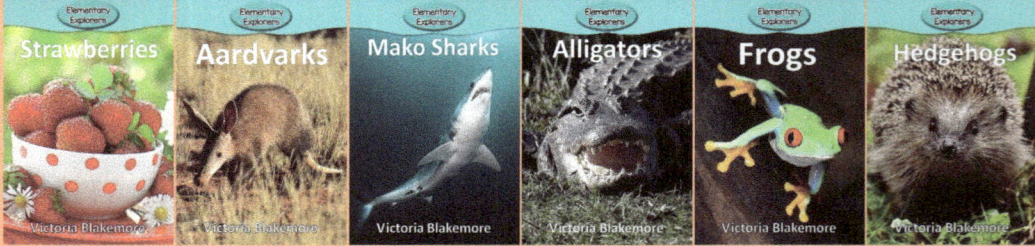

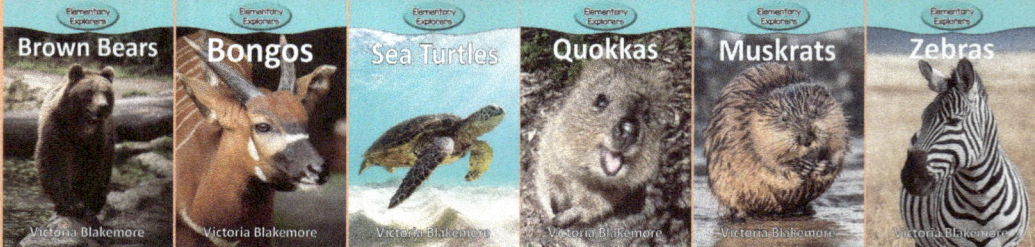

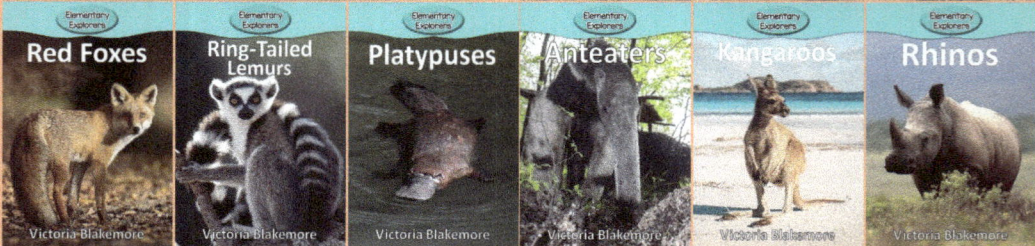

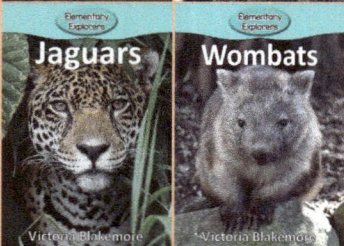

Chameleons — Victoria Blakemore
Florida Panthers — Victoria Blakemore
Aye-Ayes — Victoria Blakemore
Black Bears — Victoria Blakemore
Cheetahs — Victoria Blakemore
Manatees — Victoria Blakemore

Gingerbread — Victoria Blakemore
Polar Bears — Victoria Blakemore
Hot Chocolate — Victoria Blakemore
Orangutans — Victoria Blakemore
Coyotes — Victoria Blakemore
Marshmallows — Victoria Blakemore

Strawberries — Victoria Blakemore
Aardvarks — Victoria Blakemore
Mako Sharks — Victoria Blakemore
Alligators — Victoria Blakemore
Frogs — Victoria Blakemore
Hedgehogs — Victoria Blakemore

Brown Bears — Victoria Blakemore
Bongos — Victoria Blakemore
Sea Turtles — Victoria Blakemore
Quokkas — Victoria Blakemore
Muskrats — Victoria Blakemore
Zebras — Victoria Blakemore

Red Foxes — Victoria Blakemore
Ring-Tailed Lemurs — Victoria Blakemore
Platypuses — Victoria Blakemore
Anteaters — Victoria Blakemore
Kangaroos — Victoria Blakemore
Rhinos — Victoria Blakemore

Jaguars — Victoria Blakemore
Wombats — Victoria Blakemore

www.ingramcontent.com/pod-product-compliance
Lightning Source LLC
Chambersburg PA
CBHW051249020426
42333CB00025B/3133